Lesley Mackley

thai

simple and delicious easy-to-make recipes

This is a Parragon Book
This edition published in 2005

Parragon
Queen Street House
4 Queen Street
Bath BA1 1HE, UK

ISBN: 1-40546-232-9

Printed in China

Produced by
THE BRIDGEWATER BOOK COMPANY LTD

Photographer Simon Punter
Home Economist Ricky Turner

Cover Photography Calvey Taylor-Haw
Home Economist Ruth Pollock

NOTES FOR THE READER

- This book uses both metric and imperial measurements. Follow the same units of measurement throughout; do not mix metric and imperial.

- All spoon measurements are level: teaspoons are assumed to be 5 ml, and tablespoons are assumed to be 15 ml.

- Unless otherwise stated, milk is assumed to be full-fat, eggs and individual vegetables such as potatoes are medium, and pepper is freshly ground black pepper.

- Recipes using raw or very lightly cooked eggs should be avoided by infants, the elderly, pregnant women, convalescents, and anyone suffering from an illness.

- Optional ingredients, variations or serving suggestions have not been included in the calculations.

- The times given are an approximate guide only. Preparation times differ according to the techniques used by different people and the cooking times may also vary.

contents

introduction

Thai cooking has become increasingly popular in the last few years. Most towns have at least one Thai restaurant, and the main ingredients, which not so long ago could be found only in specialist shops, have now become widely available.

Chillies are an essential ingredient in many dishes, and if you are not used to them, add them with caution. However, the use of coconut milk and fragrant herbs and spices has a cooling effect on the heat of the chillies. It should not be difficult to find the other ingredients used in these recipes, but if, for instance, fresh lemon-grass or lime leaves are unavailable, it will not affect the recipe if dried ones are used. Lemon-grass is also available in a purée. If you find fresh lime leaves and lemon-grass, it is worth stocking up, because they freeze very well. Fish sauce is the Thai equivalent to soy sauce and is used as a seasoning instead of salt. It gives a distinctive flavour to many Thai dishes, but if it is difficult to find, use soy sauce instead.

aromatic chicken & vegetable soup
page 12

tiger prawn skewers
page 32

Many dishes in this book are suitable for vegetarians, and you can substitute soy sauce for fish sauce when the latter occurs in an otherwise vegetarian recipe.
Thai cooking can be addictive, and once you are familiar with the ingredients and able to balance different flavours, you will enjoy adapting the recipes to your own taste.

easy

Recipes are graded as follows:
1 spoon = easy;
2 spoons = very easy;
3 spoons = extremely easy.

serves 4

Recipes generally serve four people. Simply halve the ingredients to serve two, taking care not to mix metric and imperial measurements.

15 minutes

Preparation time. Where marinating or soaking are involved, these times have been added on separately: eg, 15 minutes + 30 minutes to marinate.

40 minutes

Cooking time. Cooking times do not include the cooking of side dishes or accompaniments served with the main dishes.

stir-fry chicken with thai basil
page 50

tropical fruit in lemon-grass syrup
page 86

In Thailand, soups usually stay on the table throughout the meal. They can serve as a sauce for rice or dishes that have no sauce of their own. Some soups, such as Hot & Sour Prawn Soup, are very light and can be served as a first course, whereas others are more substantial and may be served as a light lunch or supper dish. Finger food, particularly when sold on the street, is very popular in Thailand. Snacks such as Spring Rolls, Chicken Satay or Hot Chilli Relish with Crudités (Nam Prik) can be served as a starter or as party food with drinks.

soups, starters
& snacks

chicken & coconut milk soup

extremely
easy

serves 4

10 minutes   15 minutes

ingredients

400 ml/14 fl oz canned coconut milk

500 ml/18 fl oz chicken stock

6 thin slices fresh galangal

2 stalks fresh lemon-grass, bruised

4 fresh kaffir lime leaves

225 g/8 oz chicken breast fillets, cut into
 strips

2 red chillies, deseeded and sliced finely

4 spring onions, sliced finely

4 tbsp fish sauce

2 tbsp lime juice

2 tbsp chopped fresh coriander

Place the coconut milk, chicken stock, galangal, lemon-grass and lime leaves
in a large pan and bring to the boil.

Add the chicken, reduce the heat and simmer, uncovered, for 10 minutes, or until
the chicken is cooked.

Add the chillies and spring onions and simmer for 3 more minutes.

Stir in the fish sauce, lime juice and coriander and serve immediately,
in warmed bowls.

hot & sour prawn soup

very easy   serves 4–6

30 minutes   30 minutes

500 g/1 lb 2 oz large raw prawns, in shells
55 g/2 oz oyster mushrooms, sliced thinly
2 tsp light soy sauce
1 tsp white sugar
4 spring onions, sliced finely
2 tsp fish sauce
2 tbsp chopped fresh coriander

STOCK
450 g/1 lb white fish bones
2 litres/3½ pints water
2 stalks of fresh lemon-grass, chopped
  finely
2–4 small dried red chillies
4 fresh or dried kaffir lime leaves
2.5-cm/1-inch piece fresh root
  ginger, peeled
2 slices of fresh or dried galangal

To make the stock, peel the prawns and place the shells in a large saucepan with the fish bones, water, lemon-grass, chillies, lime leaves, ginger and galangal. Bring to the boil, reduce the heat and simmer, covered for 20 minutes.

Strain the stock into another large pan. Add the prawns, mushrooms, soy sauce, sugar and spring onions. Bring back to the boil, then reduce the heat and simmer for 3 minutes, or until the prawns are cooked. Add the fish sauce and coriander, cook for 1 more minute, then serve immediately.

aromatic chicken & vegetable soup

very easy   serves 4

15 minutes   30 minutes

ingredients

handful of fresh coriander
1 litre/1¾ pints chicken stock
1 stalk fresh lemon-grass, bruised
1 small fresh red chilli
grated zest and juice of ½ lime
salt and pepper

225 g/8 oz chicken breast fillet, diced
100 g/3½ oz mangetouts, cut into thin
    diagonal strips
1 carrot, shaved into ribbons
100 g/3½ oz baby sweetcorn, sliced thinly
4 spring onions, sliced thinly

Strip the coriander leaves from the stalks. Reserve the leaves and place the stalks in a large pan with the stock, lemon-grass, chilli and lime zest. Bring to the boil, then reduce the heat and simmer, covered, for 15 minutes.

Strain the stock into another pan. Add the lime juice, and salt and pepper to taste.

Add the chicken to the stock. Bring to the boil, then reduce the heat and simmer for 5 minutes. Add the mangetouts, carrot and sweetcorn and simmer for about 2 minutes, or until the vegetables are tender and the chicken is cooked.

Roughly chop the coriander leaves and stir into the soup with the spring onions. Serve immediately.

spring rolls

easy   makes 30

20 minutes   15 minutes
(food cooked
in batches)

ingredients

1 tbsp vegetable oil

250 g/9 oz lean minced pork

1 garlic clove, crushed

1 red chilli, deseeded and chopped finely

115 g/4 oz cooked prawns, shelled and
    chopped

2 spring onions, chopped finely

2.5 cm/1 inch piece fresh root ginger,
    grated finely

2 tbsp chopped fresh coriander

2 tsp fish sauce

30 spring roll wrappers

oil, for deep frying

sweet chilli sauce, to serve

Heat the oil in a frying pan. Add the pork, garlic and chillies and cook, stirring
until the pork is browned.

Add the prawns, spring onions, ginger, coriander and fish sauce. Cook, stirring,
until heated through. Remove from the heat and set aside to cool.

Prepare the spring roll wrappers as directed on the packet.

Place a spoonful of the pork mixture down the middle of each spring roll sheet,
leaving a space at the top and bottom and down the side. Brush the edges with
water. Fold the top and bottom over and then fold in the sides to form a sealed roll.

Just before serving, heat the oil for frying in a large pan or wok until nearly
smoking. Fry the rolls, in batches, for 2–3 minutes, or until golden brown.
Drain on kitchen paper and keep warm while frying the remainder. Serve with
sweet chilli dipping sauce.

chicken satay

very easy   serves 8 as a starter

10 minutes + 1 hour to marinate   10 minutes

ingredients

900 g/2 lb chicken breast meat, cut into
   5 mm/¼ inch thick, 2.5 cm/1 inch wide
   strips

MARINADE
2 tbsp vegetable oil
2 tbsp soy sauce
2 tsp tamarind paste
1 lemon-grass stalk (tender inner part
   only), chopped roughly
2 garlic cloves, crushed

1 tsp ground cumin
1 tsp ground coriander
1 tbsp lime juice
1 tsp soft light brown sugar

PEANUT SAUCE
2 tbsp smooth peanut butter
200 ml/7 fl oz coconut cream
2 tsp red Thai curry paste
1 tbsp fish sauce
1 tbsp soft light brown sugar

Thread the chicken onto bamboo skewers.

To make the marinade, place the oil, soy sauce, tamarind paste, lemon-grass, garlic, cumin, coriander, lime juice and sugar in a food processor and blend to make a paste. Transfer to a bowl.

Add the chicken to the marinade and toss to coat. Cover with clingfilm and refrigerate for at least 1 hour to marinate.

To make the peanut sauce, put the peanut butter, coconut cream, red Thai curry paste, fish sauce and sugar in a pan. Heat gently, stirring, to form a smooth sauce.

Grill the chicken on a barbecue or under a grill for 3–5 minutes on each side, or until the chicken is cooked through. Reheat the sauce, adding a little hot water if necessary, and serve with the chicken satays.

thai pork appetiser

very easy   serves 6

20 minutes   20 minutes

ingredients

4 garlic cloves, chopped finely
2 fresh red chillies, deseeded and
  chopped finely
1 tbsp chopped coriander root
1 tbsp grated fresh root ginger
3 tbsp vegetable oil
1 tbsp hot water
500 g/1 lb 2 oz lean minced pork
2 fresh kaffir lime leaves, shredded finely

2 tbsp fish sauce
1 tsp soft light brown sugar
2 tbsp roughly chopped fresh coriander

GARNISH
fresh coriander leaves
thin strips of red chilli

crisp lettuce cups, to serve

Place the garlic, chillies, coriander root, ginger, oil and water in a blender, then blend until smooth. Transfer to a wok or frying pan.

Heat and stir the paste for 4 minutes over a medium heat, then increase the heat and add the minced pork. Stir-fry for 3 minutes until coloured.

Add the lime leaves, fish sauce, sugar and chopped coriander. Continue to cook, stirring, until the pork is dry.

Serve the pork in lettuce cups, garnished with coriander leaves and strips of chilli.

hot chilli relish with crudités

extremely easy   serves 4

10 minutes   15 minutes

ingredients

RELISH

8–10 large red chillies, deseeded and
  chopped finely

6 garlic cloves, chopped finely

125 ml/4 fl oz water

½ tsp salt

2 tsp sugar

juice of 1 lime

1 tbsp fish sauce

1 tbsp vegetable oil

SERVING SUGGESTIONS

carrot sticks

radishes

cucumber batons

baby sweetcorn

Put all the relish ingredients in a pan and bring to the boil. Cover and simmer
for 10 minutes.

Transfer the mixture to a food processor and blend until smooth.

Transfer the relish to a bowl and serve with vegetables.

thai omelette

very easy   serves 2

15 minutes   30–35 minutes

ingredients

6 eggs
salt and pepper
1 tbsp butter
1 tbsp oil

FILLING
1 tbsp oil
1 small onion, chopped finely
1 garlic clove, crushed
115 g/4 oz minced pork

100 g/3½ oz green peas
2 tomatoes, peeled, deseeded and
   cut into 1 cm/½ inch dice
2 tsp fish sauce
1 tsp sugar
2 tsp lime juice
1 tbsp tomato ketchup
4 spring onions, chopped finely

salad, to serve

To make the filling, first heat the oil in a frying pan. Add the onion and garlic and fry gently for 10 minutes, or until soft. Add the pork and fry, stirring, for 5 minutes, or until coloured.

Add the peas, tomatoes, fish sauce, sugar, lime juice, tomato ketchup and spring onions. Cook, stirring, for 10 minutes, adding a little water if the mixture is too dry.

In a bowl, whisk 3 of the eggs and season with salt and pepper.

Heat half the butter and oil in an omelette pan. Add the eggs and cook for 2–3 minutes, pulling in the edges with a fork and allowing any egg to run to the base of the pan.

When almost set, place half the filling mixture on 1 half of the omelette. Fold over and transfer to a plate. Keep warm while making the second omelette. Serve with salad.

Thailand has a long coastline and a large number of the people live near the sea. They have always made use of the abundance of fish and shellfish, and Thai cuisine includes many delicious recipes for fish, prawns, crabs and mussels. Traditional Thai dishes such as Thai Fish Cakes and Prawn & Pineapple Curry are quick and easy to make using ready-made Thai fish sauce, while Tiger Prawn Skewers and Spiced Steamed Fish will liven up any dinner table.

fish & seafood

thai fish cakes

very easy   serves 4

15 minutes   30 minutes
+ 30 minutes
to chill

ingredients

500 g/1 lb 2 oz skinless, boneless cod
  fillet, cut into chunks
1 tbsp red curry paste
1 egg, beaten
1 tsp light muscovado sugar
1 tsp salt
1 tbsp cornflour
75 g/2¾ oz green beans, chopped finely
1 tbsp chopped fresh coriander

4 tbsp oil, for frying
lime wedges, to garnish

SERVING SUGGESTIONS
salad
green beans
broccoli
mangetouts

Put the cod into in a food processor and chop roughly. Add the curry paste, egg, sugar, salt and cornflour. Blend well.

Stir in the green beans and coriander.

Transfer to a bowl, cover with clingfilm and chill in the refrigerator for 30 minutes. Roll the mixture into 12 balls, then flatten each ball into a 5-cm/2-inch cake.

Heat the oil in a frying pan over a medium heat and cook the cakes in batches for about 3 minutes on each side, or until golden brown and cooked through. Keep the cooked fish cakes warm in a low oven while frying the remainder.

Garnish with the lime wedges and serve with salad or stir-fried green vegetables such as beans, mangetouts or broccoli.

prawn & pineapple curry

extremely
easy

serves 4

10 minutes

10–15
minutes

ingredients

450 ml/16 fl oz coconut cream
½ fresh pineapple, peeled and chopped
2 tbsp Thai red curry paste
2 tbsp fish sauce
2 tsp sugar

350 g/12 oz raw tiger prawns, shelled and
de-veined
2 tbsp chopped fresh coriander
4 spring onions, shredded, to garnish

steamed jasmine rice, to serve

Place the coconut cream, pineapple, curry paste, fish sauce and sugar in a pan.
Heat gently over a medium heat until almost boiling. Add the prawns and coriander
and simmer gently for 3 minutes, or until the prawns are cooked.

Sprinkle with the shredded spring onions and serve with steamed jasmine rice.

thai fish curry

easy   serves 4

20 minutes   20 minutes

ingredients

4 shallots, chopped roughly
5-cm/2-inch piece fresh root ginger,
  peeled and sliced finely
5-cm/2-inch fresh lemon-grass,
  outer leaves discarded
5-cm/2-inch fresh galangal,
  peeled and chopped finely
3 red chillies, deseeded and
  chopped roughly
1 tbsp ground almonds
½ tsp turmeric

½ tsp salt
400 ml/14 fl oz coconut cream
4 fish steaks, eg cod, turbot, halibut

GARNISH
1 red chilli, cut into thin strips
2 tbsp toasted flaked almonds

TO SERVE
cooked white rice
salad

Place the shallots, ginger, lemon-grass, galangal, chillies, ground almonds, turmeric and salt in a blender. Add 6 tablespoons of the coconut cream. Blend to a smooth paste.

Pour the paste into a large frying pan. Bring to the boil and cook, stirring, for 4 minutes. Add the remaining coconut milk and bring back to the boil.

Place the fish steaks in the pan and simmer for 10 minutes, turning once, until the fish is cooked and flakes when tested with a fork. If the sauce is too thin, transfer the fish to a heated serving dish and boil the sauce to reduce to the desired consistency. Garnish with red chilli and toasted almonds and serve with rice and a salad of your choice.

tiger prawn skewers

easy   serves 4

15 minutes   5 minutes
+ 1 hour to
marinate

ingredients

MARINADE
3 garlic cloves, crushed
2 shallots, chopped finely
2.5-cm/1-inch piece fresh root ginger, peeled
  and grated finely
1 lemon-grass stalk, chopped finely
1 fresh red chilli, chopped finely
pinch of salt

1 tbsp lime juice
1 tbsp soy sauce
2 tbsp rice wine or dry sherry
12 raw tiger prawns, in shells

GARNISH
coriander sprigs
lime wedges

3 oranges, to serve

To make the marinade, place the garlic, shallots, ginger, lemon-grass, chilli, salt, lime juice, soy sauce and rice wine or sherry in a blender and blend until smooth. Transfer to a shallow bowl.

Using a small knife, or scissors, split the prawn shells down the back, but leave attached. De-vein if necessary. Add to the marinade. Cover with clingfilm and place in the refrigerator to marinate for 30 minutes to 1 hour.

Thread each prawn onto a bamboo skewer, inserting the skewer at the tail and coming out at the head end until the pointed end extends at least 7 cm/3 inches beyond the prawn.

Grill for 2 minutes on each side, or until the prawns are pink and cooked through. Garnish with the coriander sprigs and lime wedges. Stick the skewers in the orange, to serve.

spiced steamed fish

very easy   serves 4–6

10 minutes   20–25 minutes

ingredients

2.5-cm/1-inch piece fresh root ginger, grated finely

1 lemon-grass stalk (base only), sliced thinly

6 fresh red chillies, deseeded and chopped roughly

1 small red onion, chopped finely

1 tbsp fish sauce

900 g/2 lb whole fish (eg sea bass, red snapper, trout, tilapia), cleaned

2 kaffir lime leaves, sliced thinly

2 sprigs fresh basil leaves

TO SERVE

cooked rice

cucumber batons

Place the ginger, lemon-grass, chillies, onion and fish sauce in a blender. Chop coarsely to a rough paste, adding a little water, if necessary.

Cut 3–4 deep slits crosswise on each side of the fish. Spread over the spice paste, rubbing it well into the slits.

Place the fish in a dish deep enough to hold the liquid that collects during steaming. Sprinkle over the lime leaves and basil.

Set up a steamer or put a rack into a wok or deep pan. Bring about 5 cm/2 inches of water to the boil in the steamer or wok. Put the dish of fish into the steamer or onto the rack. Reduce the heat to a simmer. Cover tightly and steam the fish for 15–20 minutes, or until the fish is cooked through. Serve with rice and cucumber batons.

fragrant mussels

easy   serves 2–3

10 minutes   15–20
minutes

ingredients

1 kg/2 lb 4 oz mussels, cleaned

2 tbsp water

1 lemon-grass stalk, bruised

2 garlic cloves, crushed

3 fresh or dried kaffir lime leaves,
  chopped roughly

200 ml/7 fl oz coconut cream

2 tbsp chopped fresh coriander

salt and pepper

warm, crusty bread, to serve

Clean the mussels by scrubbing the shells and pulling out any beards that are attached. Rinse well, discarding any that are broken or remain open when tapped.

Put the water, lemon-grass, garlic and lime leaves in a large pan. Heat until boiling. Add the mussels, cover and cook for 5–6 minutes, or until they have opened. Discard any which stay closed. Transfer the mussels to a heated serving dish, cover and keep warm in a low oven.

Boil the cooking liquid hard until reduced by half, then stir in the coconut cream. Boil to reduce and thicken slightly. Stir in the coriander and season to taste.

Pour over the mussels and serve with warm, crusty bread.

Chicken and duck are widely used in Thai cooking. Many families keep their own chickens and ducks and, because they are free range, they tend to be smaller and tougher than the ones we buy. Most recipes, such as the traditional Quick Green Chicken Curry, are quickly prepared in a wok. Pork is the most popular meat, but beef is also used in classical recipes such as Thai Beef Curry. Lamb is becoming more popular and, in most of the recipes, the meat used can be varied to suit your taste. Also in this section are main course salads made with beef or duck.

meat & poultry

grilled beef salad

very easy   serves 4

10 minutes   5–10
+ 20 minutes minutes
to soak
mushrooms

ingredients

DRESSING
2 tbsp sesame oil
2 tbsp fish sauce
2 tbsp sweet sherry
2 tbsp oyster sauce
1 tbsp lime juice
1 fresh red chilli, deseeded and
   chopped finely

600 g/1 lb 5 oz rump steak
50 g/1¾ oz dried oyster mushrooms
1 red pepper, deseeded and sliced thinly
40 g/1½ oz roasted cashew nuts

red and green lettuce leaves, to serve

mint leaves, to garnish

Place the mushrooms in a bowl, cover with boiling water and leave to stand for 20 minutes. Drain and cut into thin slices.

To make the dressing, place the sesame oil, fish sauce, sherry, oyster sauce, lime juice and chilli in a bowl and whisk to combine.

Grill the steak, either on a ridged iron grillpan or under the grill, turning once, for 5 minutes, or until browned on both sides and rare in the middle, or cook longer if desired.

Slice the steak into thin strips and place in a bowl with the mushrooms, pepper and nuts. Add the dressing and toss together.

Arrange the lettuce on a large serving platter and place the beef mixture on top. Garnish with mint leaves. Serve at room temperature.

thai beef curry

easy   serves 4

15 minutes   1½–2 hours

ingredients

3 tbsp vegetable oil

800 g/1 lb 12 oz braising steak, cubed

2 onions, sliced thinly

2 tbsp Thai red curry paste

1 tbsp tamarind paste or lime juice

2 tbsp fish sauce

850 ml/1½ pints coconut milk

2 tsp sugar

6 cardamom pods, crushed

1 small pineapple, peeled and chopped

TO SERVE

cooked rice

prawn crackers

Heat the oil in a flameproof casserole. Brown the beef in batches and set aside.

Add the onions to the oil and cook for 5 minutes, then set aside with the beef. Add the curry paste and cook gently for 1 minute, stirring constantly.

Stir in the tamarind paste, the fish sauce, coconut milk and sugar. Bring to the boil, then reduce the heat and return the beef and onions to the casserole with the cardamom.

Simmer gently, uncovered, for 1–1½ hours, or until the meat is tender. Stir from time to time and if it is becoming dry, cover with a lid.

Add the pineapple and cook for 5 more minutes. The curry should be quite dry, but add a little water if necessary.

Serve with rice and prawn crackers.

pork steaks with lemon-grass

extremely easy

serves 4

5 minutes
+ 1 hour to
marinate

10 minutes

ingredients

MARINADE
2 garlic cloves, crushed
½ tsp freshly ground black pepper
1 tbsp sugar
2 tbsp fish sauce
2 tbsp soy sauce
1 tbsp sesame oil
1 tbsp lime juice
2 lemon-grass stalks, outer leaves removed,
   chopped finely

4 spring onions, chopped finely
2 tbsp coconut milk

4 pork steaks

lime wedges, to garnish

TO SERVE
salad
stir-fried vegetables

To make the marinade, place the garlic, pepper, sugar, fish sauce, soy sauce, sesame oil, lime juice, lemon-grass, spring onions and coconut milk in a large shallow dish and mix well to combine.

Turn the pork steaks in the marinade, cover the dish with clingfilm and place in the refrigerator for 1 hour.

Grill the pork steaks under a preheated grill or over charcoal, for 5 minutes on each side, or until cooked through. Garnish with lime wedges and serve with salad or stir-fried vegetables.

tamarind pork

very easy   serves 4

15 minutes   8–10 minutes

ingredients

SPICE PASTE
4 shallots, chopped finely
2 garlic cloves, chopped finely
2.5-cm/1-inch piece fresh ginger root,
   peeled and chopped finely
1 tsp ground coriander
2 fresh red chillies, deseeded and
   chopped finely
½ tsp ground turmeric

6 blanched almonds, chopped finely
2 tbsp tamarind paste
2 tbsp hot water

2 tbsp vegetable oil
600 g/1 lb 5 oz lean pork, cut into
   thin strips
225 g/8 oz canned bamboo shoots, drained

cooked noodles, to serve

To make the spice paste, place the shallots, garlic, ginger, ground coriander, chillies, turmeric, almonds, tamarind paste and water in a food processor and blend until smooth.

In a wok or frying pan, heat the oil over a high heat. Add the pork and cook for 3 minutes, or until the meat is coloured. Then add the spice paste and continue to cook for 2 or 3 more minutes.

Add the bamboo shoots and cook for 2 more minutes, or until the pork is cooked through. Serve with hot noodles.

stir-fried lamb with mint

easy   serves 4

15 minutes   30 minutes
(food cooked
in batches)

ingredients

2 tbsp vegetable oil

2 garlic cloves, sliced finely

2 fresh red chillies, deseeded and cut
   into thin strips

1 onion, sliced thinly

1½ tbsp madras curry paste

500 g/1 lb 2 oz lamb fillet, cut into
   thin strips

225 g/8 oz canned baby sweetcorn, drained

4 spring onions, chopped finely

25 g/1 oz fresh mint leaves,
   shredded roughly

1 tbsp fish sauce

cooked rice, to serve

Heat half the oil in a wok or large frying pan. Add the garlic and chilli and cook until soft. Remove and set aside. Add the onion and cook for 5 minutes, or until soft. Remove and set aside.

Heat the remaining oil in the wok, add the curry paste and cook for 1 minute. Add the lamb, in batches if necessary, and cook for 5–8 minutes, or until cooked through and tender.

Return the onion to the wok with the baby sweetcorn, spring onions, mint and fish sauce. Cook until heated through. Scatter the garlic and chilli over and serve with rice.

stir-fried chicken with thai basil

very easy   serves 4

15 minutes   15 minutes

ingredients

2 tbsp vegetable oil

4 garlic cloves, crushed

4 spring onions, chopped finely

4 green chillies, deseeded and
   chopped finely

1 green pepper, deseeded and sliced thinly

600 g/1 lb 5 oz skinless, boneless chicken
   breast fillets, cut into thin strips

25 g/1 oz fresh Thai basil leaves,
   chopped roughly

2 tbsp fish sauce

basil leaves, to garnish

cooked rice, to serve

Heat the oil in a wok. Add the garlic and spring onions and cook for 1–2 minutes, or until soft.

Add the chilli and green pepper and cook for 2 minutes.

Add the chicken and cook until browned. Stir in the basil and fish sauce, and cook for a few more minutes, or until the chicken is cooked through. Garnish with basil leaves and serve with rice.

quick green chicken curry

extremely easy   serves 4

5 minutes   10 minutes

ingredients

1 tbsp vegetable oil
6 spring onions, sliced
600 g/1 lb 5oz skinless, boneless chicken
  breast, cut into cubes
200 ml/7 fl oz coconut cream

3 tbsp green Thai curry paste
3 tbsp chopped fresh coriander

cooked noodles or rice, to serve

Heat the oil in a large frying pan. Add the spring onions and the chicken and cook, stirring, for 3–4 minutes, or until the chicken is browned.

Stir in the coconut cream and curry paste and cook for 5 more minutes, or until the chicken is cooked through. Add a little water or stock if the sauce becomes too thick.

Stir in the chopped coriander and serve with rice or noodles.

very easy   serves 4

10 minutes   50 minutes

ingredients

2 tbsp vegetable oil
4 garlic cloves, sliced thinly
1 onion, sliced thinly
2 lemon-grass stalks, outer part removed,
  chopped very finely

2 red chillies, deseeded and chopped finely
8 chicken thighs with bones and skin
3 tbsp fish sauce
1 tbsp light brown sugar
225 ml/8 fl oz chicken stock

Heat the oil in a large frying pan. Add the garlic and onion and cook gently for 5–10 minutes, or until soft.

Add the lemon-grass and chilli and cook for 2 minutes. Add the chicken and cook for 5 minutes, or until browned all over.

Add the fish sauce, sugar and stock. Bring to the boil, reduce the heat and simmer, covered, for 30 minutes, or until the chicken is cooked through and tender. Stir occasionally and add water, if necessary. Serve immediately.

peanut crusted chicken with dipping sauce

easy   serves 6

20 minutes   35 minutes

ingredients

2 garlic cloves, crushed

2.5-cm/1-inch piece fresh root ginger,
  peeled and grated finely

1 lemon-grass stalk, outer leaves removed,
  chopped finely

2 tbsp chopped fresh coriander leaves

175 g/6 oz salted peanuts

115 g/4 oz plain flour

2 eggs

4 tbsp milk

12 chicken drumsticks, skin removed

DIPPING SAUCE

1 fresh red chilli, deseeded and
  chopped finely

2 garlic cloves, crushed

125 ml/4 fl oz white wine vinegar

2 tbsp dark brown sugar

Preheat the oven to 220°C/425°F/Gas Mark 7. Place the garlic, ginger, lemon-grass, coriander leaves, peanuts and 2 tablespoons of the flour in a food processor and blend until finely ground. Transfer to a shallow dish.

In a bowl, beat together the eggs and milk. Spread the remaining flour on a plate. Dip the drumsticks into the flour, then into the egg mixture and finally into the peanut mixture. Arrange them in an oiled roasting tin. Bake in the oven for 15 minutes, then turn them and cook for another 15 minutes. Pour off any excess oil and cook the drumsticks for 5 more minutes, or until very crisp.

To make the sauce, grind the chilli and garlic to a paste using a mortar and pestle. Put the vinegar and sugar in a pan. Heat gently until the sugar dissolves. Bring to the boil and simmer for 2 minutes. Stir in the chilli-garlic paste. Transfer to a bowl. Drain the drumsticks on kitchen paper and serve with the sauce.

roast duck salad

very easy   serves 4

20 minutes   20–30
minutes

ingredients

2 duck breasts
2 little gem lettuces, shredded
115 g/4 oz beansprouts
1 yellow pepper, deseeded and cut
   into thin strips
½ cucumber, deseeded and cut into
   matchsticks

GARNISH
2 tsp shredded lime zest
2 tbsp shredded coconut, toasted

DRESSING
juice of 2 limes
3 tbsp fish sauce
1 tbsp soft brown sugar
2 tsp sweet chilli sauce
2.5-cm/1-inch piece fresh root ginger,
   grated finely
3 tbsp chopped fresh mint
3 tbsp chopped fresh basil

Preheat the oven to 200°C/400°F/Gas Mark 6. Place the duck breasts on a rack set over a roasting tin and roast in the oven for 20–30 minutes, or until cooked as desired and the skin is crisp. Remove from the oven and set aside to cool.

In a large bowl, combine the lettuce, beansprouts, pepper and cucumber. Cut the cooled duck into strips and add to the salad. Mix well.

In a bowl, whisk together the lime juice, fish sauce, sugar, chilli sauce, ginger, mint and basil. Add the dressing to the salad and toss well.

Turn the salad out onto a serving platter and garnish with the lime zest and shredded coconut before serving.

The vegetable dishes in this section, such as Stir-fried Green Vegetables, can be served as an accompaniment to the main course or you could serve one or two of the dishes with noodles or rice as a light lunch or supper. If you omit the fish sauce, they are suitable for vegetarians. Rice is the staple food of Thailand and plain cooked fragrant rice is served at every meal. Spicy Fried Rice is a good accompaniment to a plain main course or can be served as a dish in its own right. Noodles can be combined with a wide variety of different ingredients and are equally good served hot or cold.

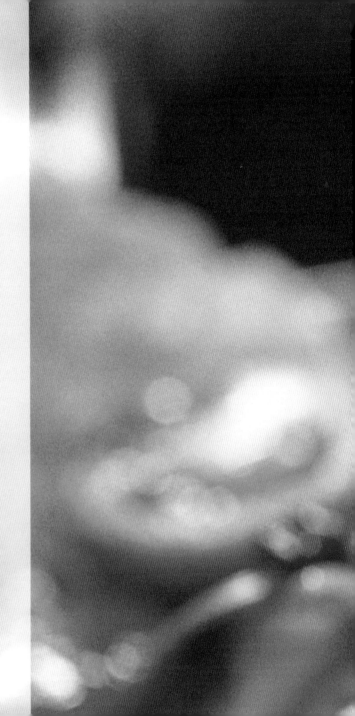

vegetables, salads, noodles & rice

stir-fried green vegetables

extremely easy   serves 4

15 minutes   10 minutes

ingredients

2 tbsp vegetable oil

3 garlic clove, sliced thinly

2.5-cm/1-inch piece fresh root ginger, sliced thinly

175 g/6 oz baby spinach leaves, washed and drained

175 g/6 oz broccoli, cut into small florets

115 g/4 oz green beans, trimmed and halved

115 g/4 oz mangetouts, trimmed and halved

freshly ground black pepper

1 tbsp fish sauce

1 tbsp oyster sauce

1 tsp sugar

4 spring onions, chopped diagonally

Heat the oil in a wok. Cook the garlic and ginger for 1 minute, then add the spinach, broccoli and beans and cook for 2 minutes.

Add the mangetouts and cook all the vegetables over a high heat, for 2 minutes.

Add the pepper, fish sauce, oyster sauce, sugar and spring onions and continue to cook for another 2 minutes.

Transfer to a heated serving plate and serve at once.

vegetable & coconut curry

easy   serves 4

20 minutes   40–50
minutes

ingredients

1 onion, chopped roughly
3 garlic cloves, sliced thinly
2.5-cm/1-inch piece fresh root ginger,
    sliced thinly
2 fresh green chillies, deseeded and
    chopped finely
1 tbsp vegetable oil
1 tsp ground turmeric
1 tsp ground coriander
1 tsp ground cumin

1 kg/2 lb 4 oz mixed vegetables (eg,
    cauliflower, courgettes, potatoes, carrots,
    green beans), cut into chunks
200 g/7 oz creamed coconut
600 ml/1 pint boiling water
salt and pepper

2 tbsp chopped fresh coriander, to garnish

cooked rice, to serve

Put the onion, garlic, ginger and chillies in a food processor and blend until
almost smooth.

Heat the oil in a large heavy-based pan, add the onion mixture and cook gently
for 5 minutes, stirring constantly.

Add the turmeric, coriander and cumin and cook for 3–4 minutes, stirring.
Add the vegetables and stir to coat in the spice paste.

In a jug, mix together the creamed coconut and boiling water and stir until
dissolved. Add the resulting coconut milk to the vegetables, cover and simmer for
30–40 minutes, or until the vegetables are tender.

Season with salt and pepper, garnish with the chopped coriander and serve
with rice.

thai salad with peanut dressing

easy   serves 4

15 minutes   10 minutes

ingredients

250 g/9 oz white cabbage, shredded
4 carrots, cut into matchsticks
4 celery sticks, cut into matchsticks
250 g/9 oz beansprouts
½ cucumber, cut into matchsticks

PEANUT DRESSING
2 tbsp smooth peanut butter
200 ml/7 fl oz coconut cream
2 tsp red Thai curry paste
1 tbsp fish sauce
1 tbsp soft light brown sugar

GARNISH
fried onion
sliced green chilli

In a steamer set above a pan of boiling water, steam the cabbage, carrots and celery for 3–4 minutes until just tender. Leave to cool.

Arrange the beansprouts on a large shallow serving dish. Arrange the cabbage, carrots, celery and cucumber on top.

To make the dressing, place the peanut butter, coconut cream, red Thai curry paste, fish sauce and sugar in a pan. Heat gently, stirring, adding a little hot water, if necessary, to make a coating sauce. Spoon a little of the dressing over the vegetables and then garnish with fried onions and sliced chilli. Serve the rest of the dressing separately.

green papaya salad

very easy   serves 4–6

15 minutes 3 minutes

ingredients

225 g/8 oz mangetouts
2 unripe papayas

DRESSING

2 garlic cloves, crushed
2 fresh red chillies, deseeded and
   chopped finely
1 tsp sugar
2 tbsp soy sauce
juice of 1 lime

GARNISH

12 cherry tomatoes, halved
2 tbsp chopped peanuts

½ head of Chinese leaves, to serve

Place the mangetouts in a pan of boiling salted water. Bring back to the boil and cook for 2 minutes. Drain into a sieve, then refresh with cold water. Cut into thin matchsticks and place in a bowl.

Peel the papayas, remove the black seeds and grate into the bowl with the mangetouts. Chill until ready to serve.

In a bowl, mix together the garlic, chillies, sugar, soy sauce and lime juice. Pour over the papaya salad and mix well.

Arrange the Chinese leaves in a large serving bowl. Put the salad on top and garnish with the halved tomatoes and chopped peanuts before serving.

pineapple & cucumber salad

very easy   serves 4

20 minutes   none

ingredients

1 cucumber

1 small fresh pineapple

1 red onion, sliced thinly

1 bunch watercress

DRESSING

3 tbsp lemon juice

2 tbsp soy sauce

1 tsp sugar

1 tsp chilli sauce

2 tbsp chopped fresh mint

Peel the cucumber and cut into quarters lengthways. Scoop out the seeds with a teaspoon and cut each quarter into 1-cm/½-inch pieces. Place in a bowl.

Peel the pineapple and cut into quarters, lengthways. Remove the core. Cut each quarter in half lengthways and cut into 1-cm/½-inch pieces and add to the cucumber. Add the onion and watercress and mix.

To make the dressing, place the lemon juice, soy sauce, sugar, chilli sauce and mint in a bowl and whisk together.

Pour the dressing over the salad and toss together. Transfer to a large serving platter and serve at once.

noodles with prawns & green peppers

ingredients

very easy   serves 4

10 minutes   10 minutes

250 g/9 oz rice noodles
1 tbsp vegetable oil
2 garlic cloves, crushed
1 fresh red chilli, deseeded and
   sliced thinly
1 green pepper, deseeded and sliced thinly
6 spring onions, chopped roughly

2 tsp cornflour
2 tbsp oyster sauce
1 tbsp fish sauce
1 tsp sugar
250 ml/9 fl oz chicken stock
250 g/9 oz small cooked prawns, shelled

Prepare the noodles as directed on the packet, drain, refresh under cold water and drain again.

Heat the oil in a wok. Add the garlic, chilli, pepper and spring onions. Cook for 1 minute, then remove from the wok to a plate and set aside.

Blend the cornflour with a little water and add to the wok with the oyster sauce, fish sauce, sugar and stock. Stir over a medium heat until the mixture boils and thickens.

Return the pepper and spring onion mixture to the wok with the prawns and noodles. Cook, stirring, for 2 minutes, or until heated through. Transfer to a heated serving bowl and serve.

fried egg noodles

ingredients

extremely
easy

serves 4

10 minutes   10 minutes

250 g/9 oz fine egg noodles
2 tbsp vegetable oil
2 garlic cloves, crushed
1 tbsp fish sauce
3 tbsp lime juice
1 tsp sugar
2 eggs, beaten lightly
115 g/4 oz cooked peeled shrimps

115 g/4 oz beansprouts
6 spring onions, sliced finely

GARNISH
2 tbsp finely chopped roasted peanuts
handful of coriander leaves
lime slices

Prepare the noodles as directed on the packet. Drain, rinse with cold water and drain again. Set aside.

Heat the oil in a wok. Add the garlic and cook, stirring, for 1 minute, or until lightly browned but not burnt. Stir in the fish sauce, lime juice and sugar and stir until the sugar has dissolved.

Quickly stir in the eggs and cook for a few seconds. Stir in the noodles to coat with the garlic and eggs. Add the shrimps, beansprouts and half the spring onions.

When everything is heated through, transfer the mixture to a warmed serving dish. Sprinkle the remaining spring onions on top and serve, garnished with peanuts, coriander leaves and lime slices.

hot & sour noodle salad

extremely   serves 4
easy

5 minutes   5 minutes

ingredients

350 g/12 oz rice vermicelli

4 tbsp sesame oil

3 tbsp soy sauce

juice of 2 limes

1 tsp sugar

4 spring onions, sliced finely

1–2 tsp hot chilli sauce

2 tbsp chopped fresh coriander

Prepare the vermicelli as directed on the packet. Drain, place in a bowl and toss with half the sesame oil.

In a bowl, mix together the remaining oil, the soy sauce, lime juice, sugar, spring onions and chilli sauce. Stir into the noodles.

Stir in the coriander and serve.

spicy fried rice

easy   serves 4–6

15 minutes 25 minutes
+ 20 minutes
to soak
mushrooms

ingredients

250 g/9 oz long grain rice
10 g/¼ oz dried mushrooms
2 tbsp vegetable oil
2 eggs, beaten lightly
2 garlic cloves, chopped finely
1 fresh red chilli, deseeded and
  chopped finely
1-cm/½-inch fresh root ginger, grated finely

2 tbsp soy sauce
1 tsp sugar
2 tsp fish sauce
6 spring onions, chopped finely
450 g/1 lb cooked, peeled small prawns
400 g/14 oz canned baby sweetcorn,
  drained and cut in half
3 tbsp chopped fresh coriander

Place the rice in a sieve and rinse under cold water. Drain thoroughly. Add the rice to a large pan of boiling salted water, bring back to the boil and cook for about 10 minutes, or until tender. Drain, rinse under cold water and drain again.

Place the mushrooms in a bowl, cover with warm water and leave to stand for 20 minutes. Drain and cut into slices.

Heat half the oil in a wok. Add the eggs. Stir the uncooked egg to the outside edge of the wok. Cook until firm. Remove the omelette, roll up firmly and cut into strips.

Heat the remaining oil in the wok, add the garlic, chilli and ginger and cook for 1 minute. Add the soy sauce, sugar, fish sauce and spring onions, stirring to dissolve the sugar. Stir in the reserved rice, prawns and sweetcorn, tossing to mix. Cook for 3–4 minutes, or until the rice is heated through. Stir in the coriander, turn into a warm serving bowl and serve at once.

Desserts other than fresh fruit are not usually served at a Thai meal, but are more likely to appear at banquets and festive occasions. The dishes in this section are delicious at any time, whether served after dinner or as a snack at another time of day. These desserts are all light and most include fruit. Tropical Fruit in a Lemon-Grass Syrup is fragrant and refreshing at the end of a meal. Coconut milk or cream are widely used in the savoury recipes in this book, but they also make creamy desserts such as the Coconut & Ginger Ice Cream and Coconut Cream Custard.

desserts

mango with sticky rice

very easy   serves 4

30 minutes   35 minutes
+ 30 minutes
to soak rice

ingredients

225 g/8 oz glutinous rice, soaked for
   30 minutes in cold water
250 ml/9 fl oz coconut milk

2 tbsp caster sugar
pinch of salt
2 large ripe mangoes

Drain the rice and rinse thoroughly. Place in a pan with the coconut milk, sugar and salt. Bring to the boil and simmer, stirring occasionally, until the rice has absorbed all the coconut milk and is very soft.

Transfer the rice to a steamer set over a pan of simmering water. Cover and steam for 15 minutes. Leave to cool a little. Spread the rice out on a tray lined with foil, then roll the rice flat with a wet rolling pin. Cut into diamond shapes.

Peel the mangoes and cut the flesh into cubes. Arrange the rice diamonds and mango cubes on individual plates or in ramekins and serve.

coconut cream custard

extremely easy   serves 4

10 minutes   20–30 minutes

4 large eggs
60 g/2¼ oz caster sugar
200 ml/7 fl oz coconut cream
1 tbsp rosewater

fresh fruit, to serve

Preheat the oven to 180°C/350°F/Gas Mark 4.

In a bowl, beat together the eggs, sugar, coconut cream and rosewater and stir until the sugar is dissolved.

Divide the custard into four ramekins. Place in a roasting tin and pour in boiling water to come half way up the sides of the ramekins. Bake in the oven for 20–30 minutes, or until set. Remove from the tin and leave to cool.

To turn out, run a sharp knife round the edge of each custard and turn out onto a serving dish. Serve with fresh fruit.

tropical fruit in lemon-grass syrup

easy   serves 4

15 minutes   15 minutes
+ 12 hours
to chill

ingredients

LEMON-GRASS SYRUP
150 g/5½ oz caster sugar
150 ml/5 fl oz water
2 lemon-grass stalks, bruised
2 kaffir lime leaves
juice of 1 lime

1 honeydew melon
1 small pineapple
1 papaya
400 g/14 oz lychees, pitted
3 passion fruit

DECORATION
1 tbsp lime zest
small handful of fresh mint leaves

To make the syrup, place the sugar, water, lemon-grass and lime leaves and lime juice in a pan. Heat gently until the sugar has dissolved. Bring to the boil and boil, uncovered, for 5 minutes. Set aside overnight.

Cut the melon in half, remove the seeds and scoop out the flesh with a melon baller. Place in a bowl. Peel the pineapple, cut into quarters lengthways and remove the core. Cut into cubes and add to the melon. Peel the papaya, remove the seeds and cut the flesh into cubes and add to the other fruit.

Add the lychees. Cut the passion fruit in half and scoop the pulp and seeds into the bowl of fruit. Stir to combine, then transfer to a serving bowl. Remove the lemon-grass and lime leaves from the syrup and pour over the fruit. Decorate with the lime zest and mint leaves and serve.

thai crêpes with papaya & passion fruit

easy   serves 4

15 minutes   20 minutes

ingredients

2 eggs
125 ml/4 fl oz coconut milk
175 ml/6 fl oz milk
115 g/4 oz plain flour
½ tsp salt
1 tbsp caster sugar
15 g/½ oz butter, melted
oil, for frying
sifted icing sugar, for dusting

FILLING
2 papaya
3 passion fruit
juice of 1 lime
2 tbsp icing sugar

In a bowl, whisk together the eggs, coconut milk and milk. Sift the flour and salt into a large bowl. Stir in the sugar. Make a well in the middle of the flour and gradually beat in the egg mixture to form a smooth batter. Stir in the melted butter.

Heat a 20–22.5-cm/8–9-inch non-stick frying pan and brush with oil. Pour in enough batter to coat the base of the pan. Tip the pan as you pour it in, so the base is evenly coated. Cook until browned on the underside and set on top, then turn the crêpe over and cook the other side. Place on a plate, cover with foil and keep warm while making the remaining crêpes.

Peel the papaya, cut in half and scoop out the seeds, reserving a few. Cut into chunks and place in a bowl. Cut the passion fruit in half and scoop the seeds and pulp into the bowl. Stir in the lime juice and icing sugar. Put a little filling on one quarter of each crêpe. Fold in half and then into quarters. Dust with sifted icing sugar. Scatter the reserved papaya seeds over and serve at once.

thai bananas

extremely easy   serves 6

10 minutes   10 minutes

ingredients

350 ml/12 fl oz coconut milk

2 tbsp granulated sugar

½ tsp salt

6 slightly under-ripe bananas, peeled and
   cut into 5 cm/2 inch lengths

1 tbsp toasted sesame seeds, to decorate

Place the coconut milk, sugar and salt in a pan and heat gently until the sugar
is dissolved. Add the banana pieces and cook gently for 5 minutes, or until the
bananas are soft but not mushy.

Divide the mixture between 6 small bowls. Scatter the sesame seeds over
and serve.

coconut & ginger ice cream

very easy

1 litre/
1¾ pints

20 minutes
+ 6–8 hours
to freeze

10 minutes

ingredients

400 ml/14 fl oz coconut milk
250 ml/9 fl oz whipping cream
4 egg yolks
5 tbsp caster sugar
4 tbsp syrup from the stem ginger
6 pieces preserved stem ginger, drained
  and finely chopped
2 tbsp lime juice

TO SERVE
lychees
ginger syrup

Place the coconut milk and cream in a medium pan. Heat gently until just beginning to simmer. Remove from the heat.

In a large bowl, beat together the egg yolks, sugar and ginger syrup until pale and creamy. Slowly pour in the hot milk mixture, while stirring. Return to the pan and heat gently, stirring constantly, until the mixture thickens and coats the back of a spoon. Remove from the heat and leave to cool. Stir in the ginger and lime juice.

Transfer the mixture to a freezerproof container. Cover and freeze for 2–3 hours, or until just frozen. Spoon into a bowl and mash with a fork or whisk to break down any ice crystals. Return the mixture to the container and freeze for 2 more hours. Mash once more, then freeze for 2–3 hours, or until firm. Remove from the freezer to the refrigerator 20–30 minutes before serving. Serve with lychees and a little ginger syrup drizzled over.

easy mango ice cream

very easy   1 litre/
             1¾ pints

10 minutes   none
+ 6–8 hours
to freeze

ingredients

600 ml/1 pint ready-made traditional
   custard
150 ml/5 fl oz whipping cream,
   whipped lightly

flesh of 2 ripe mangoes, puréed
icing sugar, to taste

passion fruit pulp, to serve

In a large bowl, mix together the custard, cream and mango pulp.

Taste for sweetness and, if necessary, add icing sugar to taste, remembering that
when frozen, the mixture will taste less sweet.

Transfer the mixture to a freezerproof container. Cover and freeze for 2–3 hours,
or until just frozen. Spoon into a bowl and mash with a fork or whisk to break
down any ice crystals. Return the mixture to the container and freeze for 2 more
hours. Mash once more, then freeze for 2–3 hours, or until firm.

Transfer from the freezer to the refrigerator 20–30 minutes before serving.
Serve with the passion fruit pulp.

index